Winter White

by Christianne C. Jones

illustrated by Todd Ouren

Special thanks to our advisers for their expertise:

Linda Frichtel, Design Adjunct Faculty
Minneapolis College of Art & Design

Terry Flaherty, Ph.D., Professor of English
Minnesota State University, Mankato

PICTURE WINDOW BOOKS
Minneapolis, Minnesota

Editor: Jill Kalz
Designer: Hilary Wacholz
Page Production: Michelle Biedscheid
Art Director: Nathan Gassman
The illustrations in this book were created digitally.

Picture Window Books
5115 Excelsior Boulevard
Suite 232
Minneapolis, MN 55416
877-845-8392
www.picturewindowbooks.com

Library of Congress Cataloging-in-Publication Data
Jones, Christianne C.
Winter white / by Christianne C. Jones ; illustrated by
Todd Ouren.
p. cm. — (Know your colors)
ISBN-13: 978-1-4048-3766-9 (library binding)
ISBN-10: 1-4048-3766-3 (library binding)
1. White—Juvenile literature. 2. Colors—Juvenile literature.
I. Ouren, Todd, ill. II. Title.
QC495.5.J667 2008
535.6—dc22   2007004272

The world is filled with COLORS.

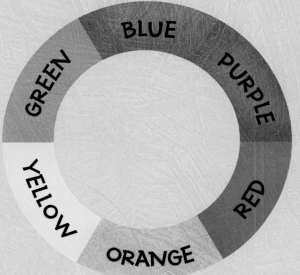

Colors are either primary or secondary. Red, yellow, and blue are primary colors. These are the colors that can't be made by mixing two other colors together. Orange, purple, and green are secondary colors. Secondary colors are made by mixing together two primary colors.

White and black are neither primary nor secondary. They are neutral, or achromatic, colors. They are used to tint other colors, or make them darker or lighter. To make a color lighter, add white. To make a color darker, add black.

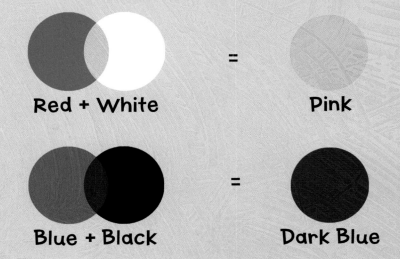

Red + White = Pink

Blue + Black = Dark Blue

3

The color **WHITE** can be fluffy and cold.

A snowy wonderland is a sight to behold.

Sparkling **WHITE** snowflakes cover the ground.

A sleeping WHITE owl won't make a sound.

8

9

Bright **WHITE** clouds stretch long and wide.

10

11

A cozy **WHITE** igloo is a fun place to hide.

A chubby WHITE snowman wears a black hat.

14

Sticky **WHITE** snowballs fly fast and go SPLAT!

WHITE figure skates glide on the rink.

Tasty **WHITE** cream tops a warm drink.

21

It's time to go in. The air has a chill.

You can look for more **WHITE** from the windowsill!

TINTING WITH WHITE

WHAT YOU NEED:
- red, yellow, and blue paint
- paper plates
- white paint
- paintbrushes

WHAT YOU DO:
1. Put a quarter-sized blob of red paint on a paper plate.
2. Add a few drops of white paint to the red, and mix the colors together with a brush.
3. Repeat the first two steps with the yellow and white paint, then the blue and white. How do the colors change?
4. Now, try the activity again. This time, add just one drop of white paint to each color. How does the amount of white paint affect the colors?

FUN FACTS
- The color white usually stands for things that are pure, clean, and innocent.
- In many parts of the world, white is the color that brides wear. In other parts of the world, white is used at funerals.
- Ivory, alabaster, and cream are all words that mean "white."
- Raising a white flag is a sign of surrender, or giving up.

TO LEARN MORE

AT THE LIBRARY
Dahl, Michael. *White: Seeing White All Around Us.* Mankato, Minn.: Capstone Press, 2005.
Parker, Victoria. *White with Other Colors.* Chicago: Raintree, 2004.
Whitehouse, Patricia. *White Foods.* Chicago: Heinemann, 2002.

ON THE WEB
FactHound offers a safe, fun way to find Web sites related to this book. All of the sites on FactHound have been researched by our staff.

1. Visit *www.facthound.com*
2. Type in this special code: 1404837663
3. Click on the FETCH IT button.

Your trusty FactHound will fetch the best sites for you!

Look for all of the books in the Know Your Colors series:

Autumn Orange
Batty for Black
Big Red Farm
Brown at the Zoo
Camping in Green
Hello, Yellow!
Pink Takes a Bow
Purple Pride
Splish, Splash, and Blue
Winter White

24